MW00571694

1001 Puns, Dad Jokes, and One-Liners

TH Leatherman

1001 Puns, Dad Jokes, and One-Liners by TH Leatherman

Published by Fivefold Publishing LLC, PO Box 586, Firestone, CO 80520.

ISBN: 978-1-7353990-1-0

ACKNOWLEDGEMENTS

My first Thank You is to you. Thank you for loving jokes and being the kind of person that makes the world a brighter place. To my wife, who puts up with my morning routine, with cries of, "What?" and "Why do you do this to me first thing in the morning?" and "Oh my god, please get me a cup of coffee before you do that." Your patience truly has no bounds. Thanks to my sons, Drake and Ashton, for being an appreciative audience. Your groans and eye rolls feed my soul every day. Special thanks to the members of the Crafty Writing Monkeys and if you have an adverse opinion on the jokes in here, raise your hand then put it over your mouth. To Saytchyn Maddux-Creech, you did it. We both know you did it. We'll never speak of it again.

Special thanks also to Merrilee Leatherman, Kat Kane, Dan Bergman, Carol Stratton, Becca Valencia, Marvin Andrews, Katrina Watts, J T Evans, Jim Bartlemay, Brian Hirsch, Bonnie Garrett, Cassandra Kelly, Bobert Lizak, A K Caggiano, Sito Sainz, Paul Clark, Kelyn Walker, Zach Johnson, Dacia Arnold, Shannon Creamer, Dave Rooda, Lacey Bright, Kate Jonuska, Aimie Runyan, (deep breath) Patty Sanchez, Rebecca Rowley, Allynn Riggs, Kelyn Walker, Clair Fishback, Amy Armstrong, DeAnna Knippling, Felicia Frantz, Mike Nash. Mitch Newstadt, Stephanie Reisner, Ken Kroeger, Heather Cooper, Aften Brook Szymanski, John Robey, Quill Mueller, Thea Hutcheson, Rod McCormac, and Geno Jorgensen, and way too many more people to name here. Oh, and Kelyn Walker. Your support helped me inflict my jokes on a wider audience. You should be ashamed of yourselves.

FORWARD

(because three -ward and five-ward didn't sound right)

This book is dedicated to Dads everywhere. We have a tough job. Not everyone can kill spiders, reach the top shelf, or sacrifice their body so that our mate can warm their butt against us. Over the years we've become adept at tea parties, clapping wildly at every performance, and hunting down every misplaced dish or light left on. We've accused everyone else of losing the remote, quoted every movie that no one ever watched, and lost games just to see their smiles.

But most of all, we've been there to lighten the load. We've wiped away every tear, consoled every fear, and held those we hold dear. And because we're dads, we tell jokes. The good, the bad, and the unfunny. Through every groan and covered face, through every sigh and head shake, we've been there for those we love. We do it because we see the giggles and smiles when they think we're not looking. We do it because our home should be a place where they can feel safe. Jokes make a house a home, filled with laughter and love.

This book is for you dads. Because bad puns are how eye roll.

CONTENTS

(or mal-contents, after all it's a book of bad jokes)

1 ANIMAL AND INSECT PUNS

I took my friend's dog for a walk. It was the leashed I could do.

How Squirrels prepare for the winter, it's nuts!

My dog is so gangsta. All about the pug life.

My dog was blowing his coat, so I dropped him off at the groomers. Then I went home to clean. Gone, but not fur-gotten.

My dog is my fur-ever friend.

The secret to life is belly rubs. Jasmine, dog philoso-fur.

Dog puns make me bark with laughter.

What's better than a spelling bee? A talking dog!

Some dogs like to surf. You can find them in Colliefonia.

Dog puns have so much pet-tential.

My dog likes my girlfriend. She's mutts about him too.

My dalmatian likes bacon treats. They really hit the spot.

My puppy loves doggie day care. It's a paw-ty everyday.

My dog never stands up for herself. She always rolls over.

My dog's puppies are so messy. A bunch of litter pugs.

I took my dog to the flea circus, and he stole the show!

Raining cats and dogs is fine, as long as it doesn't reindeer.

My best friend petted all the hair off my dog. It was hard to fur-give him for that.

My terrier is so scary, we call him the big bad woof.

My dog is very big on safety. He insists everything go to the lab for testing.

Greyhounds are good at telling tall tails.

Getting a new dog is a lot of work. I'm glad my job has pup-ternity leave.

What do you call a dark Eskimo dog? A dusky husky.

My dog loves the internet. She's a Cyber-ian Husky.

My dog will dive underwater for treats. He's a subwoofer.

My husky has a chronic illness. Irritable Howl Syndrome.

I named my dog Frost. Frost bites.

My dog nearly walked out the door, but we renegotiated the terms of his leash.

My dog likes my garden. I can tell because he digs it.

Veterinarians know how to make dogs heel.

When my friend told me to stop acting like a flamingo, I had to put my foot down.

What's a snake's favorite subject. Hiss-tory

Snails aren't faster without their shells. They're more sluggish.

My Dad saw a bunch of rabbits walking backward. A receding hare line.

Shaving crazy sheep is shear madness.

What do you call a deer with no eyes. No-eye-deer.

Cows wear bells because their horns don't work.

Giraffes take a while to apologize. It takes a long time to swallow their pride.

Horses stay thin by being on a stable diet.

Crabs don't share. They're shellfish.

A man was rushed to the emergency room with six plastic horses in his stomach. Doctors described his condition as stable.

I watched a beaver documentary last night. Best dam show ever.

Noah kept the bees in the ark-hives.

An alligator in a vest is called an investi-gator.

Bees. Working hard for their honey.

Bring your pet to work day. My boss brought a hamster. I brought a red tail. Talk about hawkward.

Whenever a kitten cuddles up to me, I want to whisker away.

The best way to communicate with fish is to drop them a line.

Cows with two legs are lean beef.

I chicken proofed my lawn. It's impeccable.

Cows keep the grass short. They're lawn mooers.

Petting cats leaves me feline good.

I don't like insects. They really bug me.

Fish live in salt water, because pepper water makes them sneeze.

My horse fell, now he can't giddyup.

A horse lives next door to me. He's my neigh-bor.

Watch dogs keep the best time.

Dogs can't dance because they have two left feet.

Ducks make the best detectives. They always quack the case.

Rabbits are fun pets. They're always hoppy to meet you.

Bunnies prefer beer with lots of hops.

Never pay a pelican to be your fishing guide. Their bills are enormous.

A cow got into the pot field. The steaks have never been higher.

My overweight parrot died. I'm sad but it's a huge weight off my shoulders.

Where do fish keep their money? In a river bank.

People who take care of chickens, are chicken tenders.

Why do fish sing off key? Because you can't tuna fish.

Butterflies. They're not what they used to be.

When you're down by the sea and an eel bites your knee, that's a moray!

Horses are happy because they live in a stable environment.

A friend of mine told me a bird pun, and I thought toucan play at that game.

Spotted cats are always broke, because cheetahs never prosper.

I can't tell cow jokes. I butcher it every time.

Leopards are bad at hide and seek. They're always spotted.

Two silkworms had a race. It ended in a tie.

Oysters don't share their pearls because they're shellfish.

I haven't seen my fish friends lately. I should drop them a line.

The big cat relationship was doomed from the start. He was a lion, and she was a cheetah.

Pay no attention to the pachyderm in the room, It's ir-elephant.

Is that your dog? No, we were unable to conceive a dog naturally, its adopted.

A chicken crossing the road is poultry in motion.

Pig puns are boaring.

Bears without bees are just ears.

My dog gave birth in a park and was fined for littering.

Cuddling cats, leaves you feline good.

Chickens hate the end of the week. Fry-day.

Chicken farms are multi-layer organizations.

I was told it takes five sheep to make one sweater. I didn't know they could knit.

My dog has an attitude. He's a cocky spaniel.

I used to breed chickens, but I couldn't make hens meet.

Two snails got in a fight. Once the shells came off, it was a real slug fest.

Those that believe in giving drugs to animals should get off their high horses.

At the circus, the lion hairstylist was the mane attraction.

When dogs finish obedience school, they go for their masters.

Deer who can use all hooves equally well are bambidexterous.

It must be hard for bats to sleep upside down, but I guess they get the hang of it.

A cowboy got a horse for his birthday. That night he read it a story. It destroyed a couch. Never book a gift horse in the house.

I asked to borrow a dollar from a horse, but she only had fore quarters.

The way squirrels prepare for the winter, it's nuts!

My friend wanted to tell me a squirrel joke. I told him to go nuts.

My dog loves the canine news, but she's busy, so she listens to a pawed cast.

I caught the bird flu. I'm a victim of fowl plague.

Obstetricians and storks do have one thing in common, a large bill.

If birds of a feather stick together, they must be vel-crows.

I'm concerned about my neighbor the shepherd. As soon as he enters the field, the sheep make an ewe turn.

Some animals at the aquarium got loose. It was otter chaos.

She claimed it was an alligator purse, but I knew it was a crock.

Dairies are rarely robbed. Cow are used to beef up security.

Sheep take forever to get to the point. They always bleat around the bush.

Birds never know where they're going. They're always winging it.

My dalmatian hides whenever he needs to go to the vet. It's not a problem though. He's always spotted.

Scotsmen now have their own site for posting videos. Ewe Tube.

I enjoy wool gathering for the shear joy of it.

My wife made venison for dinner. Oh deer.

The stork doesn't deliver all babies. Heavier ones require a crane.

The dog race was called on account of fleas. It had to be scratched.

There are a lot of spiders in my garage. It's a no fly zone.

I took a test on apiaries. I got a bee on it.

Bugs are religiously diverse. They're all in sects.

Calves take well to bottle feeding. One nipple is as good as an udder.

The long shot horse was in the lead at the beginning of the race, but it didn't last furlong.

Bears sometimes fight each other over territory. The results are often grizzly.

You can own too many dogs. It's called a roverdose.

I got a cat even though I'm allergic. It was a rash decision.

I got a pig so we could hunt mushrooms, but he's more truffle than he's worth.

Aladdin has an animal companion. It's a flying carpet.

Moths have good lives because they always look for the bright side.

What's the saddest dog? A melon-collie.

Watch your step after its been raining cats and dogs. You might step in a poodle.

The year of the dog was a ruff one for me.

My dog is famous. We're always avoiding the pup-arazzi.

Some days my greyhound can't catch a rabbit. Those are the bad hare days.

My dog is cute. Quite fetching, really.

My puppy always wants to go on a walk. She's dog-matic about begging for them.

When I go out of town, my dog stays at puppy motel. It's very pawsh.

There were so many dogs at the picnic, it became a Bark-B-Q.

Pitchers fear my dog. He's always getting walked.

My favorite dog book is Hairy Pawter and the Terrier's Bone by JK Growling.

Pavlov? That rings a bell.

My dog is an expert at playing fetch, he can give you a few Pointers.

I like my beer like I like my rabbits. With lots of hops.

My chickens were upset when their home was destroyed, but they'll recoup.

I've never tipped a cow before, but also a cow has never served me food.

Some dogs are good with locks: Corg-keys.

My dog never answers robo-calls. He has collar ID.

My wife asked why we don't go out anymore. I pointed to the dog and said, "What do you mean? We have whining and dining every night."

My wife asked if we could get another dog. I said, "Sure, go mutts."

To everyone who has enjoyed my dog puns, "Thank you very mush!"

The most popular pet among lumberjacks is the timber wolf.

I saw a dog adopted by a wealthy couple today. It was a true wags to riches story.

When killer whales sing, it's orcastrated.

Eagles can catch mice because they're talon-ted.

Laughing stock. Cattle with a sense of humor.

I love my dog so much I spend more in his haircut than I do my own.

2 JOBS AND SPORTS PUNS

Taking ore is a load off someone's mine.

The firewood industry revolves around its axes.

I had a cavity, but my regular dentist was sick.
It was fixed by a guy who was filling in.

Why did the teacher wear sunglasses to school?
She had bright students.

What kind of underwear do astronomers wear?
Fruit of the moon.

Vegans may think that butchers are awful, but people selling vegetables are grocer.

I got a new job making chess sets. I'm on knights next week.

Electricians need to strip, to make ends meet.

How did the pirate get his ship? It was on sail.

How do you have a party for astronomers? You planet.

Are calls at SeaWorld recorded for training porpoises?

Seismologists are paid to predict earthquakes. Doesn't that make them a faults prophet?

I saw a nun wandering around our neighborhood. She must be a roamin' Catholic.

Old skiers, go downhill fast.

The news said a silent street performer was killed. A mime is a terrible thing to waste.

Two conspiracy theorists walk into a bar. You can't tell me that was a coincidence.

I do a lot of resistance training, by not going to the gym.

An unemployed Jester is nobody's fool.

The doctor gave me a neck brace. I haven't looked back since.

Cleaning mirrors. That's a job I can see myself doing.

I was fired from making calendars. All I did was take a day off.

A caricature artist was arrested today. The details are sketchy.

A clinic with two doctors has a pair a docs.

Rumor has it that my boss is firing people with bad posture. I have a hunch, it might be me.

I once dated a philosophy professor. I don't know if she knew I existed or not.

Fishermen are reel men.

At my new job, I have 500 people under me. It's a cemetery, but still.

I used to work as a lumberjack, but I couldn't hack it, so they gave me the axe.

Students who cut class, are absent minded.

I entered a stair climbing competition. Now I need to step up my game.

My Dad was fired from being a road worker for stealing. I didn't believe it, but when I got home, the signs were all there.

I build stairs for a living. It's an up and down business.

I thought about plumbing while I slept. It was a pipe dream.

I used to recycle shoes, but it was sole destroying.

When lawyers become cooks, they're a sue chef.

The tree trimmers did a good job. I told them to take a bough.

Electricians are always up on current affairs.

I used to advise a demolitionist. It was destructive criticism.

The carpenter showed up this morning to install a door. He made a grand entrance.

Obstetricians. Celebrating Labor Day, every day.

A lot of pilots are really out there but find piloting drones to be too remote.

Never date a tennis player. Love means nothing to them.

I don't do archery. Too many drawbacks.

I watched a long movie about Japanese sword fighters. Let me samurais it for you.

Every martial arts crime fighter needs a good sidekick.

Check out clerks ask paper or plastic because baggers can't be choosers.

It has been my life long vision to be an optometrist, but I can't see a way to make it happen.

Because I can use two typewriters at once, I get accused of stereotyping.

Electricians go with the flow, not against the current.

Jokes about pole vaulters never go over well.

Installing mufflers is exhausting work.

CSI searched for blood evidence, but it was all in vein.

The priest canceled the prophecy class due to unforeseen circumstances.

Jogging makes you feel better in the long run.

Splitting the price of a taxi is fare.

My dentist became a prosecutor. Now he extracts the truth.

Paratroopers pull strings to stay on the job.

Can anyone tell me, is the delivery business picking up or dropping off.

When there are earthquakes, geologists are quick to find fault.

Farming cotton is a classic story of good versus weevil.

I like my landscaper. He's easy to get a lawn with.

I lost my tarot cards. It made me sad. They cost a fortune.

Being a waiter isn't the greatest job, but it puts food on the table.

Real estate agents have a lot to talk about.

I won a sewing competition. I guess I should quilt while I'm ahead.

Since I've quit football, I've lost my goal in life.

My relationship with my Uber driver isn't going anywhere. It always feels like he's driving me away.

Taxidermy is for stuffy people.

Cobblers are always looking for sole mates.

I climbed the hill of higher learning only to be knocked centless by a mountain of debt.

A locksmith is a key employee.

For back pain, I thought I'd take a stab at acupuncture. My appointment is this afternoon and I'm on pins and needles.

When job hunting, look deep inside. It's all about the inner view.

The museum art curator had an eye for fine paintings. She displayed art official intelligence.

I like chiropractors. They always have your back.

A sommelier serves wine, but it's a pour job.

Programmers don't like the outdoors. Too many bugs.

Farmers really know how to party. They really get down when the beet drops.

There are a dozen baseball fields in my hometown. That's just a ballpark number.

Some couples don't go to the gym. Not every relationship works out.

I'm addicted to somersaults, but that's how I roll.

My tailor was happy to make me a new suit. Or at least sew it seams.

My insurance doesn't cover acupuncture. I got stuck with the bill.

In the recent market correction, the scuba industry really took a dive.

There was a line out the door for the hairdresser, and I thought, "What a great day for a barber queue."

A sword swallower was found dead at the circus. Police suspect it was an inside job.

Never tell a podiatrist how many meters you walked. They only understand feet.

I'm the best at playing Twister. Hands down.

Coin collectors get together for old dimes sake.

I got a new job in cartography. It's really going to put me on the map.

Cleaning windows is a real pane.

Historians are masters of extra-century perception.

My son had a class trip to a soda bottling factory. At the end there was a pop quiz.

I dropped out of my communism class because of lousy Marx.

I got a job at a bakery. I kneaded the dough.

Be nice to your dentist. He has fillings too.

After years with the same chiropractor, I saw a new one. It was quite an adjustment.

The coffee tasted like mud, but the barista said it was ground this morning.

Butcher puns don't make the cut.

Seamstresses always keep extra thimbles. You never want to be stuck without one.

Glue salesmen stick to their word.

Since I've taken the job in the everglades, I've been swamped.

After waiting hours for the bowling alley to open, we finally got the ball rolling.

Jewel thieves are hard to catch, if they have a good ring leader.

My skiing skills have really gone downhill.

The idea of wearing a helmet goes over my head.

I lost my new sales job. Now I have to vend for myself.

As a journalist, I visited Greek ruins. I needed material for my columns.

Two kayakers were cold and started a fire. The boat sank. You can't have your kayak and heat it too.

Farming is a growing industry.

I just received my permit to catch small shrimp. It's a license to krill.

There was a fire at the shoe factory. A thousand soles were lost. Some heel did it while he was laced.

I took a job as a gift wrapper. I'm presently employed.

I've been a jogger for four years running.

I dropped out of cartoon class. I'm now in suspended animation.

Two florists got hitched. It was an arranged marriage.

I'm starting a rope tying business. It's a knot for profit organization.

I wanted to be a marine biologist, but I couldn't keep my grades above C level.

It was great being a watchmaker. I got to make my own hours.

My wife says I'm addicted to golf. She says it's driving a wedge between us.

My friend installs ceiling fans. He was always a screw up.

Some people play softball. That's a very underhanded thing to do.

Pilots can always find work. They're great at landing jobs.

Reassembling prehistoric skeletons can be a mammoth job.

Electricians get supplies from the outlet store.

I was caught between making a salad or playing catch with my son. It was a toss up.

Yoga teachers don't lie, but sometimes they stretch the truth.

You brought a non-regulation puck to the hockey game, but we'll let it slide.

I found a spotter at the gym. That's a huge weight off my shoulders.

I work in a sweater factory. It's a clothes knit community.

You never see fat painters. They're always using thinner.

Optometrists live a long time. They dilate.

I wanted to go camping, but we couldn't get the tent up. Too many missed stakes.

Baking is for early risers. They make most of their dough at yeast before leaven o'clock.

Forklift operators don't make Dad jokes. They find them unpalletable.

I work in a cement factory. My job keeps getting harder and harder.

Woodworking test today. Nailed it!

I used to date a telephone operator, but she had too many hang ups.

I used to have a fear of hurdles, but I got over it.

I used to do a lot of rock climbing in my twenties, but I was much Boulder back then.

My florist is crazy. She makes flower derangements.

After last year's alpine skiing medalist took a bad fall, it was all downhill from there.

Conditions at the fencing company were bad. The workers formed a picket.

Long distance runners with bad shoes suffer the agony of de-feet.

Teachers who don't take attendance are absent minded.

I used to teach computer science, but I lost my drive.

The globe means the world to geography teachers.

My physics teacher was out today. Gone fission.

Sensitive pickpockets take things personally.

Heavy breathing while stretching can lead to yoga pants.

Shout out to baseball players after three strikes.

I saw a show on how ships are put together. Riveting.

I've decided not to invest in mortuaries. It's a dying business.

Mimes are determined to remain silent, to say the least.

I tried to learn coding, but I couldn't get with the program.

My doctor suggested a lobotomy to relieve stress and I thought, "That's a no-brainer."

Becoming a podiatrist is no small feet.

A dressmaker can never have enough fabric, at least sew it seams.

I got angry when my cell phone died. My Psychologist suggested I find an outlet.

My wife has a business selling almonds. She also has a delivery guy. He drives her nuts.

Judges that drone on and on give long sentences.

My golf ball landed ten feet off the fairway, but that's a rough estimate.

I couldn't remember the last time I exercised, so I went for a run, to jog my memory.

I applied for a casino job, but they didn't have a slot for me. It was a bit of a gamble anyway.

I love meteorology, but I have to admit, most of it is over my head.

I know a hacker. He goes on a lot of phishing trips.

My electrician is very smart. He knows what's watt.

What does a carpenter do after one night stand? A second nightstand.

I don't like my masseuse. She rubs me the wrong way.

I want to do some mountain climbing, so I'm working out. I need to be in peak condition.

I meant to exercise today, but it didn't work out.

Do people who climb the highest mountain Ever Rest?

I became a fisherman for the halibut, but floundered, and couldn't live off the net income.

I'm working at the sleep clinic. It's my dream job.

I became a phone service rep. It was my calling.

The psychic two doors up went out of business. I wonder if she saw it coming.

Embroidery needles and Darning needles will never see eye to eye.

Cotton farmers never die, they just bale out.

My friend, the manicurist, went back to school to become a vet. She was great at giving a pet a cure.

Say what you will about hangmen, they're great at communication. Always keeping people in the loop.

Scuba diving is a great way to get in over your head.

As my Dad said, as one door closes, another one opens. Great man. Terrible cabinet maker.

My Optometrist said my glasses are ready. I'm not sure if I believe him, but we'll see.

It's hard for prospectors to get a drink. Most bars don't serve miners.

I was kicked out of mime school. I think it was something I said.

I used to work in a factory making bras, but it went bust.

I’ve been itching, but I think going to a dermatologist would be a rash decision.

Shouldn’t people who install carpet be called floorists?

3 SCIENCE AND MATH PUNS

I wanted to clone
my brain
But I realized I was
getting a head of myself
thleatherman.com

You never hear about how Pterodactyls went to the bathroom. Because the P is silent.

Advanced geometry isn't too hard. It's as easy as pi.

There's a new book about faster than light travel. It's bound to take you somewhere.

I went to examine the Barringer site in Arizona. I wanted to see it in crater detail.

Time travel jokes are so funny. I'll laugh at them again, and again, and again...

This is the sandpaper of the future. Real science friction.

Why don't physicists major in time travel? There's no future in it.

Oxygen and Potassium went out on a date. It was OK.

Absolute zero is OK with me.

All the good chemistry jokes Argon.

In biology, multiplication and division are the same thing.

In chemistry most problems are a solution.

My microbiologist friend travels around a lot. He's a man of many cultures.

I hate it when blood cells fall in love. I know it's all in vein.

Sometimes light goes bad and ends up in prism.

When I tell chemistry puns, I'm in my element.

Ugh, I hate dealing with electrons. They're always so negative.

I like chemists. They have all the solutions.

I think I left Bromine and Boron in the cabinet, BrB.

I broke the law of gravity and got a suspended sentence.

If my lab smells like rotten eggs, I apologize for your sulfering.

Plants don't like math. It gives them square roots.

I wasn’t sad when my flashlight batteries died. I was delighted.

You can’t have flowers, if you haven’t botany.

There a fine line between a numerator and a denominator. Only a fraction of people will get this joke.

I said to myself, the cloning machine worked!

I love the way the earth rotates. It really makes my day.

I started to boil water, but when I came back it was gone. I mist it.

When I feel blue, I remind myself to breathe again.

Oxidation, the reason I have rust issues.

Don't call people average. That's just mean.

To the mathematician that discovered zero: thanks for nothing!

I'm reading a book on antigravity. It's impossible to put down.

I wanted to make a joke about sodium, but Na...

I found a rock yesterday that was 5280 feet long. It was a milestone.

I was born a pessimist. My blood type is B negative.

If the US switched from pounds to kilograms, there'd be mass confusion.

My body is a prison, made up of cells.

I have problems with math, but chemistry gave me solutions.

Mermaids are good at math. It's all the algebras.

I just found out they won't be making yardsticks any longer.

Something about subtraction doesn't add up.

Geometry shapes my life.

Why do people care so much about pi day? It's so irrational.

I make chemistry jokes periodically.

Never ask mathematicians about pi. They go on and on.

I can't understand my calculus teacher. He talks in sine language.

I love WiFi. We have that kind of connection.

If global warming is causing sea levels to rise, does that mean that oceans are getting too big for their beaches?

Books about black holes, really draw me in.

People think I'm square, but I'm right from every angle.

Periodically, chemists feel out of their element.

Albert Einstein got along great with his cousins, relatively speaking.

I watched a thunderstorm to understand lightning. Then it struck me.

I looked up impotence on the internet, but nothing came up.

My geometry class was always tired. They were all out of shape.

Some numbers can't sit still. Those are the roamin' numerals.

I once went on a date at an internet café. We didn't click.

There's a new drug that makes you angry. It's all the rage.

I took a class on statistical probability. It was average.

I developed a new theory on inertia, but it isn't gaining any momentum.

It's time to upgrade my bed with a new comforter. I need to get with the program and get one down loaded.

Global warming is a heated topic.

Some atoms misbehave. You have to keep an ion them.

People who plug keyboards into iPods aren't stupid. That would be stereo typing.

Math books have problems.

Bacteria walks into a bar and the bartender says that they don't serve bacteria. The bacteria says, "But I work here. I'm staph."

Atheists don't solve exponential equations. They don't believe in higher powers.

I'm all about geometry, but graph paper is where I draw the line.

You can find the best place to use a colon by process of elimination.

I bought a new computer and they threw in an operating system to boot.

Scientists expected the volcano to blow, but it didn't. It suffered eruptile disfunction.

An educated tube is a graduated cylinder.

Length times width times height speaks volumes.

Hamburgers have less energy than steaks. They're in a ground state.

My lamp told me that electrons turn it on.

I trust my calculator. It's something I can count on.

I live in an area with earthquakes, but I refuse to let them shake me.

Gravity makes me sad. Always pulling me down.

Recharging batteries is revolting.

There are three types of people in the world, those that can count and those that can't.

Some puns make me feel numb, but math puns make me feel number.

6:30 is the best time on the clock, hands down.

Scientists have grown vocal cords in a Petri dish. Results speak for themselves.

I asked to borrow my friend's chloroform. He said, "Go ahead. Knock yourself out."

4 GRAMMAR AND WRITING PUNS

I got a job at a prison library
It has its prose and cons
thleatherman.com

How many grammar nazis does it take to screw in a lightbulb. Too.

I'm friends with 25 letters. I don't know Y.

I wrote a book on basements. It made the best cellar list.

Reading while sunbathing makes you well red.

Double negatives are a no-no.

Arguments about word puzzles involve crosswords.

A book fell on my head. I have only my shelf to blame.

Thanks for explaining the word many to me. It means a lot.

I'm reading a story in Braille. Something bad is going to happen, I can feel it.

A semicolon broke the grammar laws and was given two consecutive sentences.

I'm glad I learned sign language. It's pretty handy.

Dark is spelled with a K because you can't C in the dark.

Borrow books from your library, but don't overdue it.

Ghost writers lift the spirits of their readers.

I'm reading a romance in Braille. It's a touching story.

I'm reading a book on machine oil. It's non-friction.

The meaning of opaque is unclear.

My neighbor who stole my journal has died. My thoughts are with his family.

Rejection is all about who you no.

When you see an improper lowercase letter, capitalize on it.

Sperm cells look like commas and apostrophes because they interrupt periods, and lead to contractions.

I had my appendix removed. I'll never be able to reference this chapter of my life.

If I wrote a book about birds, would it fly off the shelf?

I asked the librarian if she was free this afternoon. She said she was booked.

My wife is concerned about my obsession with puns. I told her it's a phrase I'm going through.

I planned on publishing a book about sinkholes, but it fell through.

The tallest building in any city is the library. So many stories high!

I was looking for a catchphrase to fight illiteracy, but words failed me.

Punctuation: the difference between a sentence that's well written, and a sentence that's, well, written.

My next book: How to Fall Down a Staircase, A Step by Step Guide.

So what if I don't know what apocalypse means. It's not the end of the world.

We talked about the past, present, and future. The conversation was tense.

Cleverness is one way to judge a pun, but other have groan in significance.

I hate cliff hangers. Do you know what I'm going to do about it?

I went to a theatre for Phantom of the Pun. I expected a big production, but it was just a play on words.

Copyright law is a statute of imitations.

I had an original idea for a book. It was a novel thought.

Hyperbole is without a doubt the single most amazing thing that has ever happened to the earth.

I wrote a book about a small garden, but there wasn't much of a plot.

A noun and a verb were dating, but the verb broke it off. The noun was too possessive.

I know I could learn Braille once I got the feel of it.

My friend went out with a girl named Simile. I called it date, he said it was more of a get together, a meeting, or a rendezvous.

There was a scandalous rumor that Shakespeare also owned a bakery. There was much ado about muffins.

I wrote a story about a tornado. There's a twist at the end.

As a Dad, I enjoy a good play on words. To my wife, it's just pun-ishment.

"That's what." -She

A bunch of vowels and consonants appeared in court today. They're due to be sentenced next week.

Autocorrect. My arch enema.

My friend asked if someone could name two pronouns. I said, "Who, me?"

Never invite John Milton to game night. There's always a pair a dice lost.

I thought the run-on sentence might be pregnant. The period was late.

Writing poetry should be left to the prose.

My wife yelled, "can't, won't, wouldn't, couldn't," so I took her to the hospital. She was obviously having contractions.

Cats have claws at the ends of their paws. Commas have a pause at the end of their clause.

I'm not versed in writing songs. I refrain from it.

I took a creative writing class after a friend recommended it to me. I had a simile experience.

Years ago, I thought about writing a Civil War book, but it was gone with the wind.

When writing beer recipes, you need to have a first draft.

Writing long stories, that's a novel idea.

Avid readers don't have extra time. They're always booked.

I caught my dog eating a book. I took the words out of his mouth.

I fell in love with a good book. It was bound to happen.

I read a book on orange juice. It was pulp fiction.

I could never have a date with a library book. People are always checking them out.

I was involved in a secret library project. It was very hush-hush.

Witches make good editors. They know all about spell check.

Some authors are downright spooky. Those are the ghost writers.

Library carts sometimes stay out all night. That's how they roll.

My friend raved on and on about Lord of the Rings. That's what I'm Tolkein about.

Books are good for dates. They always have a great opening line.

The Divinyls are great for book lovers. When I think about their music, I touch my shelf.

JK Rowling almost made a book about Harry's godfather. She didn't go through with it because it was too Sirius.

How do you track down a good book? You follow their footnotes.

Charles Dickens' food was always hit or miss because of his spices. He had the best of thymes and the worst of thymes.

I wrote a book about motor oils. It had no frictional characters.

I know a writer who used to be a mobster. He was an author I couldn't refuse.

I took a book with me into surgery, to have the appendix removed.

Plots are important. They build character.

Anyone remember where the water was on Animal Farm? Was it in a pond Orwell?

Ghosts make the best readers. They go through books quickly.

I don't like periods. They're always telling me to stop.

Books make brave warriors. They have spine!

I know how many books I have. I'm very shelf aware.

I'm dating a librarian. She's got really great books.

Students are very aggressive. Always hitting the books.

There's one word that's shorter when you add two letters to it. Short.

I saw a book about phobias, but I was afraid it wouldn't help me.

As much as I enjoyed the book, I had to leave it. She'd never open up to me.

I always take a second look at a good book. It deserves a re-view.

Cops are big readers. If you don't pay the fine, they book you.

Books on Podiatry have footnotes. Books on Proctology have endnotes.

I read a book on Stockholm Syndrome. The first chapters were horrific, but by the end I could relate to it.

I had plans to read a book on sinkholes, but they fell through.

It's hard to date a librarian. They're always booked.

Music teachers often get into trouble for encouraging students to read band books.

I thought a had a sketch book around here, but I'm drawing a blank.

I started to read a book about mazes, but I got lost in it.

I'm a librarian and a detective. I solve bookcases.

I read poetry books backwards. Inverse.

Broken pencils are pointless.

The days of calendars are numbered.

As Steinbeck said, hangovers are the Wrath of Grapes.

If you cook alphabet soup long enough, it spells disaster.

Cowboys write poetry because their inspired by moos.

Poets don't like commercials because they're ad-verse.

Hanging is too good for punsters. The must be drawn and quoted.

I went to a theater performance about puns, but it was just a play on words.

How do writers change a lightbulb? They screw it almost all the way in, then give a surprise twist at the end.

The president's speech writer has resigned. He's speechless.

I dreamt I was in the Lord of the Rings, but my wife says I was Tolkien in my sleep.

Grammarians are never late. They're always punctual.

The pencils raced across my desk. It was a draw.

Why did I become an editor? Well, to cut a long story short...

I was traumatized after losing my editing job. I suffered post-grammatic stress disorder.

Irony. The opposite of wrinkly.

People who don't know the difference between etymology and entomology bug me in ways I can't put into words.

Become a thespian today. Act now.

I asked a librarian for a book on Pavlov's dog and Schrodinger's cat. She said it rings a bell, but she didn't know if they had it or not.

Grammarians may be vowel friends, but they're consonant professionals.

Nostalgia isn't what it used to be.

5 PUNS ABOUT MONEY

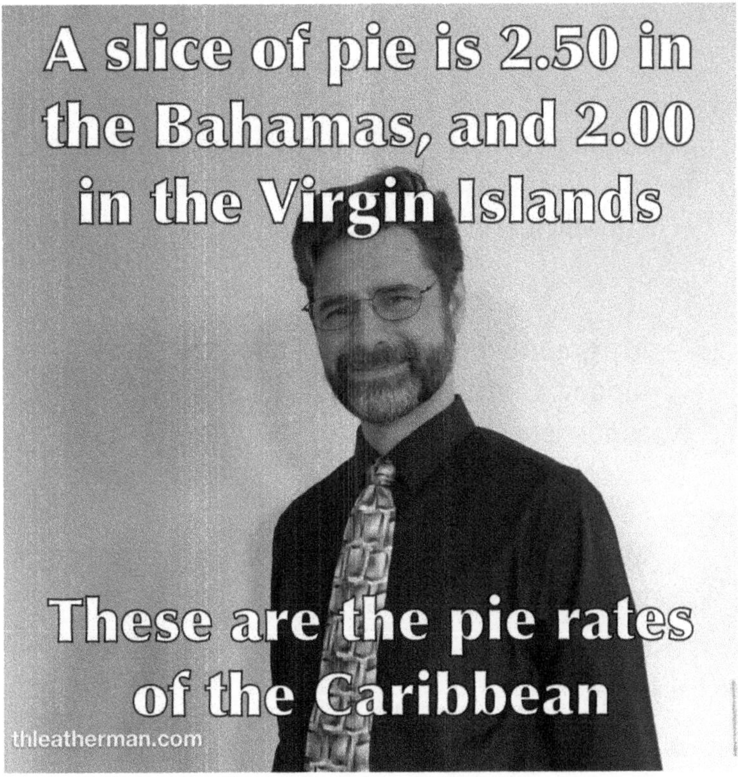

A slice of pie is 2.50 in the Bahamas, and 2.00 in the Virgin Islands
These are the pie rates of the Caribbean
thleatherman.com

My landlord asked to speak with me about the heating bill. I told him my door was always open.

I used to be a banker, but I lost interest.

Interest has an accrual way of accumulating.

A compass manufacturer had a shareholder meeting. Investors were concerned the company wasn't heading in the right direction.

Some people invest in precious metals like gold or silver. Which is better? It's an either ore situation.

My grade school bully still takes my lunch money. On the bright side, he makes great sandwiches.

Money isn't everything, but it sure keeps you in touch with your kids.

Money talks, but all mine ever says is goodbye.

Think nobody cares about you? Try missing a couple of payments.

I've studied the economy, the best time for me to buy a car was last year.

College is the opposite of kidnapping. They demand payment or they'll send your kid back to you.

When my first child went off to college, I felt a great emptiness. In my savings account.

I'm so broke, I can't even pay attention.

I've put something aside for a rainy day. An umbrella.

If money grew on trees, everyone's favorite season would be Fall.

I remember being so broke that I couldn't afford my electric bill. It was a dark time.

Materialism: Buying things we don't need, with money we don't have, to impress people that don't matter.

I have all the money I'll ever need... If I die by 5 pm.

Money can't buy happiness, but it's more comfortable to cry in a Porche than a bicycle.

I have an unlimited cell phone plan. There's no limit to what they can charge me.

I need a new bank account. This one has run out of money.

It's not hard to meet expenses. They're everywhere.

Credit Cards are very dangerous. Every time I use one, my wife chases me with scissors.

Money is the root of all wealth.

The best way to get back on your feet is to miss a couple of car payments.

Born free. Taxed to death.

Interviewer: Why do you want this job? Me: I've always been passionate about not starving to death.

When I say I'm afraid of the dentist, I mean the bill.

My wife and I are serious about planning for retirement. We're playing the lottery every chance we get.

Money can't buy happiness, but it makes misery easier to deal with.

My nephew swallowed coins and was rushed to the hospital. I called my brother and he said there was no change yet.

Homeless accountants stay in tax shelters.

The baker's accounts weren't quite right. He fudged the numbers.

A banker fell overboard during a cruise. He was okay though. He could float a loan.

My bank went out of business in the last earthquake. It fell into default.

One company makes the game Monopoly.

The book that has helped get the most out of life is my checkbook.

If time is money, then ATMs must be time machines.

At the bank, a woman asked me to check her balance. I pushed her over.

My professor said I was failing my ethics class, so I slid him a twenty.

There are lots of scams out there, but for five payments of $19.95, I'll show you how to avoid them...

I keep eating fortune cookies, but so far, I'm not rich.

I spent a lot of money to rent a limousine, but then it didn't come with a driver. I can't believe I spent so much and have nothing to chauffer it.

The coin press at the US mint stopped working and no one can figure out why. It just doesn't make cents.

The balloon shop is closing. They couldn't keep up with inflation.

The most honest President was Lincoln. He was in a cent.

Ten cents isn't worth as much these days because the dimes have changed.

6 PUNS ABOUT OUTER SPACE

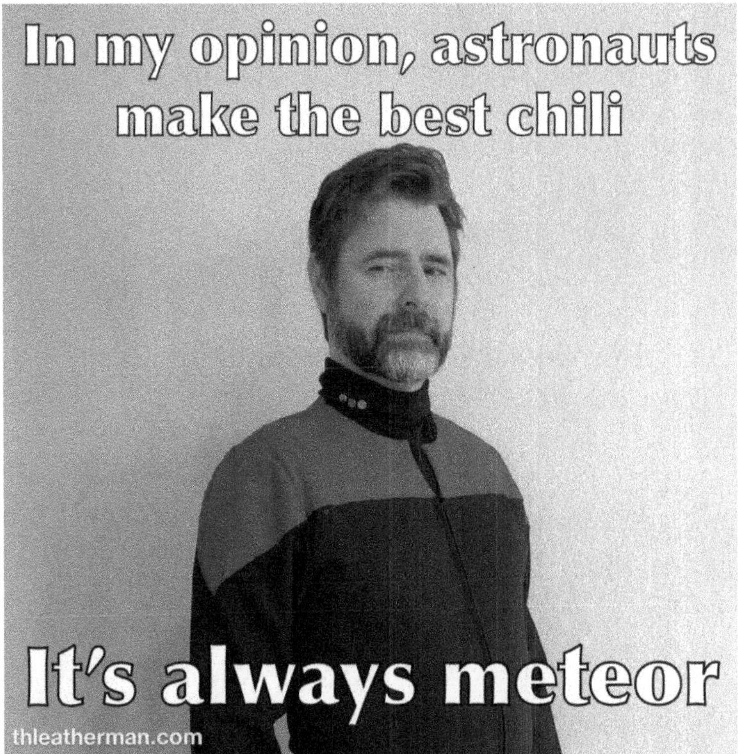

How does the man in the moon cut his hair? Eclipse it!

Jupiter holds up its pants with an asteroid belt.

Living on Earth is expensive, but it includes an annual free trip around the sun!

Why would you send a clock to the moon? You'd have to be a lunar-tick.

The moon is almost broke. It's down to its last quarter.

Space poems are written in uni-verse.

How does the sun greet us in the morning? Pleased to heat you!

What does the sun bring on a trip? A light snack.

Did you know that there's a restaurant on the moon? Great food, but no atmosphere.

I stayed up all night wondering where the sun went. Then it dawned on me.

How do you put baby planets to sleep? You rocket.

Why don't aliens visit us? Terrible ratings. One star.

Meteor showers rock my world.

I was delighted by the solar eclipse.

The sun asked the moon why he was so down. He told her it was just a phase.

I tried to research when an alien spaceship came to earth, but it was over my head.

What is ET short for? He has tiny legs.

What is a lightyear? Like a regular year but with fewer calories.

Astronauts aren't hungry after blasting into space. They've just had a big launch.

Astronauts prefer to drink gravi-tea.

A wizard on a spaceship is a flying sorcerer.

Aliens park their saucers at a parking meteor.

What do you call an alien with three eyes. Aliiien.

A spaceship with a water leak is a crying saucer.

He didn't win the Shaw Prize for Astronomy, but he did win a Constellation prize.

The sun never needs to go to college. It already has a million degrees.

I know a guy who's crazy about the moon. A real lunar-tic.

7 SCIENCE FICTION PUNS

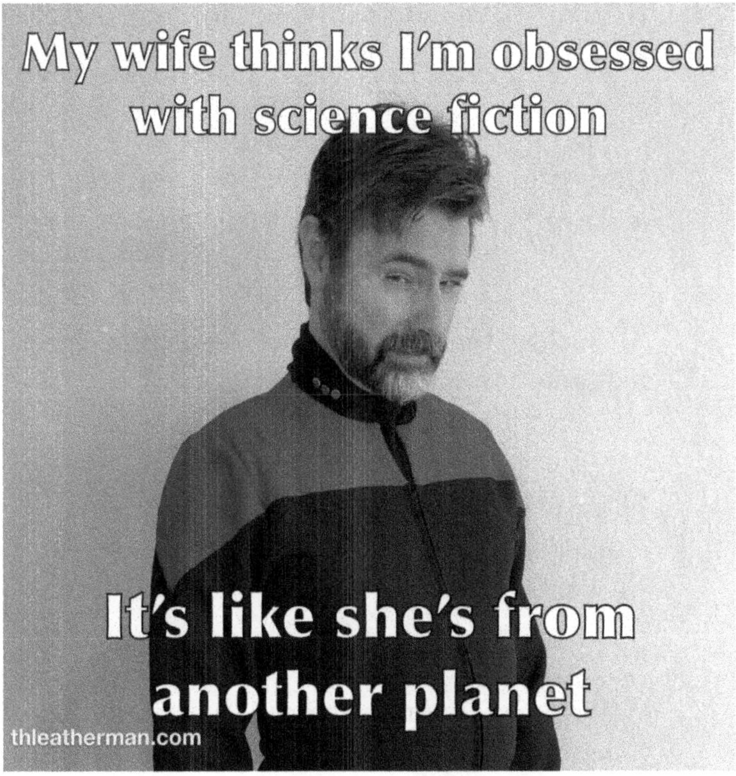

My wife thinks I'm obsessed with science fiction
It's like she's from another planet
thleatherman.com

I asked Master Yoda about fixing the light panels in the Jedi temple. He said clone Han Solo, you must. Many Hans make light work.

You know that movie where Charlton Heston comes back to a planet full of wines. Planet of the Grapes.

In 2001, Dave went to Jupiter, for the HAL of it.

During an experiment, a flock of geese got loose on the station. It was a wild goose space.

Aliens love the mile-high city. It's a little closer to home.

The Earth is being invaded by mutant dandelions. Their demands: Take me to your weeder.

Why are Sci-fi puns so great? They're out of this world.

My wife asked me to dress up as a bounty hunter. She has a Boba Fetish.

There's a word for too many aliens at a sci-fi convention. Extra Terrestrials

Only 7 of 9 Star Trek Voyager jokes are funny.

You're traveling at dusk through a garden of not only sight and sound, but also the mind. There's a signpost ahead - The Twilight Gnome.

How come you never see two Doctor Who's? Because it would be a Pair-a-Docs.

I just drove in from a Transformers convention, and boy my arms are tires.

Did you know that Anakin Skywalker wanted to become a country singer? He almost changed his name to Darth Brooks.

Princess Leia couldn't find Obi-Wan, because she was looking in Alderaan places.

Why don't you see many Darth Vader toys anymore? They're a choking hazard.

Sith don't change light bulbs. They prefer the dark side.

What do you call a Jedi with no eyes? Jed.

Jedi never go drinking with Yoda, because he doesn't pay the tab. He's always a little short.

Why do Jedi Knights always use analogies? Because metaphors be with you.

Aliens need their space.

If time travelers are still hungry, they go back four seconds.

Dogs don’t become Jedi Knights because they’re easily seduced by the bark side.

What do you call a man with no arms or legs in a volcano? Anakin Skywalker.

The small furry aliens said they came from the Dog Star. I thought, “They can’t be Sirius.”

8 FANTASY AND PIRATE PUNS

I'm never afraid of the dark
Wherever I am, it's always Knight time
thleatherman.com

I asked the Captain how he got his hook. It was an off hand comment.

A jousting match lasts, until knight falls.

Demons are a ghouls best friend.

Long fairy tales tend to dragon.

Campaigns during Christmas are Advent-tures.

How much does pirate corn cost? A buccaneer.

How do trees get on the internet? They log in.

I met a wizard who liked to turn things into glass. I asked why, and he said he just wanted to make things clear.

Introverted Hobbits are shyer folk.

Dwarves have very little in common.

I saw the movie Shrek. It was ogre rated.

Never trust a rogue. They're all backstabbers.

They filled in the canal around the castle. It was demoated.

It's hard to take pictures of fairies because they're pixie-lated.

Never give gold to a sick fairy, it's most likely a leper-con.

You can't bake fairies. You have to put a gnome on the range.

Fairies are graded on a scale. They get points for elf improvement.

There are lots of fairy sightings in Las Vegas. It's all the elvish impersonators.

The drug store lost Cinderella's pictures. Not to worry though, someday her prints will come.

I met a girl wearing a cloak and cussing at people. Little rude riding hood.

Cinderella is bad at soccer. Always running away from the ball.

I'm not sure what possessed me to attend a séance.

Did you hear the tooth fairy got arrested? It was for incisor trading.

A warlock threw a teacup at me. I should have expected it from a Tei-fling.

Pirates are good singers because they can hit the high seas.

Everyone loves hit points, they're the life of the party.

A thief was stealing from a camp of traveling mistrals. They chased him to a cliff and caught him between a rock and a Bard place.

Be wary of priests that don't heal and ask enemies to sign waivers. Those are desk clerics.

Bards avoid getting hit because they have high 'amour' class.

Buford was an awful vampire, so he decided to do poetry as well. He went from bat to verse.

Musicians should always warm up before a performance to avoid minstrel cramps.

Robin Hood used arrows to get his point across.

When player characters die, they roll in their graves.

Small hairless lizard creatures? They must be ko-balds.

I don't like being a peasant, but resistance is feudal.

Pirate ships are very efficient. They get thousands of miles to the galleon.

Why is pirating so addictive? Because after you lose a hand, you're hooked.

The dread pirate Bluebeard fell overboard in the Red Sea. He got Marooned.

9 FOOD PUNS

There was a fight at a seafood restaurant
Battered fish were everywhere
thleatherman.com

I went for coffee and found that my biscuits were stolen. I will find them. I will leave no scone unturned.

Coffee has it rough at my house. Always getting mugged.

Why did the banana go to the doctor? He wasn't peeling well.

I prefer my kale with a silent K.

Beer is a gateway drug for aspirin.

My relationship with whiskey is on the rocks.

If you are what you eat, I must be super sweet.

If you know any vegetable puns, lettuce know.

Crushing cans is soda pressing.

French pancakes give me the crepes.

I ordered 2000 pounds of Chinese soup. It was a won ton.

I wrote a song about tortillas. Actually, it's more of a wrap.

I lost my poker chips, so I used dried fruit instead. People went nuts when they saw me raisin the stakes.

I'm happy with my new fridge magnet. Now I have a dozen fridges.

People become butchers to meat people.

Where does spaghetti dance? The meatball.

When your bread gets good grades, it's an honor roll.

I won the costume contest 5 years in a row dressed as a sandwich. I'm on a roll.

My waiter asked how I found my steak. I told him it was easy. It was right next to the potato.

Smoking will kill you. Bacon will kill you. But smoking bacon will cure it.

I tell everyone about the benefits of eating dried grapes. It's all about raisin awareness.

An explanation of an acorn. In a nutshell, it's an oak tree.

Butchers link sausage to make ends meat.

I used to make doughnuts for a living, but I became fed up with the hole business.

Food prepared on guard duty, can last for sentries.

Pizza jokes are cheesy.

You don't see bread at weddings. They prefer to e-loaf.

I get distracted by the meats in the deli section. I have a short attention spam.

Jokes about peanut butter are wide spread.

Tomatoes blush because they saw the salad dressing.

I asked the waitress if my pizza would be long. She said no, it would be round.

I accidentally drank food coloring. The doctor says I'll be fine, but I feel like I've dyed inside.

My wife made me clock cookies. It was very time consuming.

Inferior dumplings are a sign of wanton neglect.

Pork leftovers are ham me downs.

Ever since the romaine lettuce recall, its been really hard to get a head.

Lab grown meat is silly. Why reinvent the veal?

The word doughnut has a certain ring to it.

I thought pancakes sounded good this morning, but I kept waffling.

Newtons are my favorite snack. Go fig.

Eating oysters helps increase mussel tone.

I wanted leftovers, but it wasn't meant to be. Foiled again.

My best friend and I like to cook together. We're taste buds.

The trick with grapes is raisin them right.

The butcher didn't have enough turkeys for the holiday, so he asked customers to bid on them. They complained, but auctions speak louder than birds.

There's a new restaurant called golfers. All courses come with greens.

My friend's son ate all the Italian pastries. I cannoli imagine what he's going through.

This bunch at the vineyard was really juiced. They kept wine-ing about their one moment of grapeness.

They had bright lights at the Chinese restaurant. I asked them to dim sum.

It just hit me. Tofu is overrated. It's just a curd to me.

Passing by the deli everyday makes me crave sandwiches sub-consciously.

You can always find yogurt at an art exhibit. It's cultured.

The right beer is a very personal choice. Decide on a case by case basis.

Stir fry cooks come from all woks of life.

The high cost of birthday cake blew me away.

My friend's pantry is full of jelly. It's jam packed.

My onions have started singing hip hop, the little rap scallions.

My circumference is too big. Too much pumpkin pi.

Corn shells fall apart easily, but we don't taco bout it.

Naked bananas lack a peal.

Don't use 'beefstew' as a password. It's not stroganoff.

10 MISCELLANEOUS PUNS

Protesting is all well and good
But vandalism is only a stone's throw away
thleatherman.com

My daughter brought a talking doll to church. It was a weapon of mass disruption.

I discussed rights and lefts with my ex. She was right, so I left.

Did you hear the joke about three holes? Well, well, well...

Trees love the spring. They're re-leafed.

If at first you don't succeed, skydiving is not for you.

I make apocalypse jokes, like there no tomorrow.

Mountains aren't just funny, they're hill areas.

To be Frank, I'd have to change my name.

Walking in high heels keeps my wife on her toes.

Elevator music bothers me, on so many levels.

I met a woman with a taser. Man she was stunning.

Pro tip: Never take sleeping pills and laxatives at the same time.

Not all seasons are the same. Summer warmer than others.

My mood ring is missing. I don't know how I feel about that.

At first I didn't like having a beard, but then it grew on me.

When I was younger I robbed a kitchen. I was a whisk taker.

The least spoken language in the world is sign language.

My wife got me a get better card. I'm not sick, she just thinks I can do better.

An underwear bandit was caught. He confessed to a brief crime spree.

Some people are wise. Other people are otherwise.

Shout out to my fingers. I can always count on them.

He who laughs last. Didn't get it.

Ancient Romans gathered once a week. That was enough forum.

I have a friend who's half Indian. Ian.

I want to be a ghost for Halloween. I better get my sheet together.

Can't get up to vote? You must have electile dysfunction.

I scream, you scream, the police show up, it's awkward.

Where there's a will, there's a relative.

What lies at the bottom of the ocean and twitches? A nervous wreck.

I'm a big fan of whiteboards. I find them remarkable.

I used to have a soap addiction, but I'm clean now.

Needles to say, I hate syringes.

My wife likes it when I blow in her ear, but honestly I'm not a fan.

I thought about making a belt of watches, then I realized it was just a waist of time.

I just found out I'm colorblind. The diagnosis hit me right out of the purple.

I saw an ad for burial plots, and I thought, that's the last thing I need.

Writing with a broken pencil is pointless.

For Halloween we dressed up as almonds. Everyone said we were nuts.

My doctor said not to worry about bird flu. It's tweetable.

I'm selling my vacuum cleaner. It was just collecting dust.

Children avoiding nap time are guilty of resisting a rest.

With great reflexes, comes great response ability.

I wanted to learn to procrastinate, but I never got around to it.

Have you tried the new reversable jackets. I'm excited to see how they turn out.

I hate peer pressure, and you should too.

A bike can't stand on its own. It's two tired.

When I get naked in the bathroom, the shower gets turned on.

I couldn't remember how to throw a boomerang, then it came back to me.

The best time to open a gift, is the present.

I got a universal remote, and I thought, this changes everything.

Someone stole my limbo stick. How low can you get?

My cousin got caught stealing a calendar. He got 12 months.

My wife says I'm addicted to skin lotion. I said, go ahead, rub it in.

I wondered why balls look bigger when they're thrown at you. Then it hit me.

I asked my sister why she was crying. She told me she was having a cry-sis.

I was surprised to see the snowman at the bike race. He was riding an icicle.

Fixing broken windows is a pane in the glass.

Scarecrows are outstanding in their field.

Someone stole everything but my soap, shampoo, and towels. The dirty bastard.

I used to be afraid of Santa Claus. But I got over being Claustrophobic.

Broken drums make great Christmas gifts. You can't beat them.

Santa's helpers are subordinate Clauses.

Santa uses chimneys, because it soots him.

My dyslexia has hit a new owl.

Everyone needs something to believe in. I believe I'll have another drink.

I have an odd talent to tell what's inside a wrapped box. It's a gift.

I asked my Christmas lights why they stopped working. They told me they were burnt out.

I got my son a fridge for Christmas. I can't wait to see his face light up.

Ocean puns are deep.

Every house needs a door. That's where I come in.

I can't help being lazy. It walks in my family.

Claustrophobic people think better outside the box.

Waking up is an eye-opening experience.

I tripped over my wife's bra. It was a booby trap.

I have a photographic memory, but I never developed it.

Sleeping comes naturally to me. I can do it with my eyes closed.

My friend went bald but still carries a comb. He just can't part with it.

The best way to capture skeletons is with a rib cage.

My zipper broke, but I fixed it on the fly.

I was overcharged on Velcro. What a rip off.

Tractors are magical. I saw one turn into a field.

It took me a long time to learn how to use a seatbelt. Then one day, it just clicked.

At first, I didn't like duct tape. Then I became attached to it.

The way gems are made is crystal clear to me.

It's never wise to take quartz for granite.

Bidding on silent auctions is not aloud.

Rumpled clothing is a pressing issue, but I can iron out a solution.

I love puns about eyes, The cornea, the better.

I haven't cleaned the floor in a while. It's suffering from sweep deprivation.

Can I tell you some chimney jokes? The first one is on the house.

The couch in my den is a remote location.

I love the wind. It blows me away.

I didn't think wearing orthopedic shoes would help, but I stand corrected.

My friend said, "Cheer up, you could be in a hole filled with water." I know he means well.

Baby spoons are delivered by a spork.

I got new Chapstick. It's the balm!

I told my wife it was her turn to shovel the walk. All I got was an icy stare.

Itching for bargains. Try the flea market.

When it comes to maternity puns, I deliver.

I collect vintage time pieces. I have a watch list.

I got caught in the freezing rain. It hurt like hail.

Alternative facts are aversion of the truth.

I have an angry watch. It's always ticked.

Rashes developed from swine flu and can be treated with oinkment.

My friend put honey in my weapons locker. He denies it, but I'm sticking to my guns.

Silence is golden, but duct tape is silver.

Nails are priced per pound.

Where do mansplainers get their water? From a well, actually.

I changed all my user names to Kenny. Now I have Kenny logins.

My kids play hopscotch everywhere, but my driveway is where I draw the line.

I couldn't get out of bed this morning, but I'll recover.

When you buy a cork board, do you pay a thumb tax?

Wounds heal better when covered. An example of gauze and effect.

Jokes about labyrinths are a-mazing.

Jokes about floating, don't go down well.

My son failed his coloring exam. I gave him a shoulder to crayon.

A case of weight loss pills was stolen. Suspects are still at large.

A sleeping bag is also a nap sack.

Corduroy pillows, they're making headlines!

We want dirtbags to clean up their act, but they insist on living in a vacuum.

My glasses steamed up, and I don't know why. I was misti-fied.

He who steals the sheets is wrapped up in themselves.

I'm teaching my slinky new tricks. It's spring training.

I expected my first elevator ride to be uplifting, but it really let me down.

My ice house fell apart, but don't worry. Igloo it back together.

My wife accused me of farting, but I told her I was in a scent.

I asked my wife if she enjoyed doing laundry. She replied, “Loads.”

I don’t compost. It’s degrading.

Do nudists give each other bare hugs?

I’m adding sinks to every room. I’m trying to become multi-fauceted.

Never trust stairs. They’re always up to something.

I hear my mothers voice telling me to do the right things. It’s my inner mom-ologue.

My mother always helped me be my best. She was my opti-mum.

Air travel fees are getting ridiculous. On my last flight they charged me for my emotional baggage.

When choir robes are too long, they need to be hymned.

My girlfriend tried on some tight jeans, but she couldn't pull it off.

Some people take beautiful pictures and cut them to pieces. It's a puzzle to me.

My wife tinted her hair. It was the highlight of her day.

I wanted to buy a camouflage shirt, but I couldn't find one.

They said I had type A blood, but it was a typ-O.

I used to think I was indecisive, but now I'm not so sure.

Vandals attacked a parking garage. It was wrong on so many levels.

There was a trampoline sale at the sporting goods store. Needless to say, I jumped on the offer.

Great stores never close. They just sale away.

The results of a can-do attitude are candid.

I love my lawn today. I'll love it mower tomorrow.

I'm a wine enthusiast. The more I drink, the more enthusiastic I get.

My wife says I'm a skeptic, but I don't believe her.

The price of comforters is on the rise. The cost of down is up.

I was late because I had to go to the bathroom. I was stalling.

Weight loss mantra. Fat chants.

I didn't know she had dentures, until it came out in conversation.

I heard a joke about amnesia, but I forgot how it goes.

I used to meditate a lot, but now I only do it now and zen.

I turned an old quarry into a parking lot. Since then, I've had a lot on my mine.

I have a relief map of downtown. It shows where the restrooms are.

Why did I pass out? I haven't the faintest idea.

I've never taken an elevator to a basement. It's beneath me.

The furniture store keeps calling me wanting me to spend more time with them, but all I wanted was one nightstand.

Towels tell jokes, but most people don't understand them. They have a dry sense of humor.

I saw something similar to moss yesterday, but I don't know what I'd lichen it to.

I just watched a horror movie that comes out next month. It was a private screaming.

The forest looks less stressed this Spring. Even the trees look releafed.

I like elevators. They're very uplifting.

The Y claimed to house two thousand campers. That seems like a lot of bunk.

On a recent visit to Hawaii, I was surprised by all the highways. For a moment I thought I was in road island.

After being condemned, workers started up the wrecking ball, and razed the business to a new level.

The old pine admonished the sapling for being knotty.

I bought a new bush trimmer. It's cutting hedge technology.

Insomnia, I'm getting tired of it.

I have a fear of needles. They get under my skin.

I met my girlfriend when she backed into me. We met by accident.

My cousin was sentenced to death but got a stay of execution. No noose is good noose.

I thought my feet would be arch enemies, but it turns out they're sole mates.

The cost of funerals has risen significantly. I blame the high cost of living.

I bought a book on phobias. I'm afraid of reading it.

I saw a misprint of 'The Game of Lfe', and I thought, 'it's all fun and games until someone loses an I.'

You know that origami store? It folded.

I wanted to learn to drive a stick, but I couldn't find the manual.

I didn't trip. I attacked the floor!

People who gossip have a sense of rumor.

Atheism is a non-prophet organization.

I told my family I quit smoking for the holidays. Did I get everything I wanted? Clothes, but no cigar.

Taking things literally can be confusing, but at the end of the day, 11:59.

My vacuum broke in the middle of cleaning. I can't tell if it sucks or not.

Time flies when you're throwing alarm clocks.

Monarchs worry about receding heir lines.

When I was young, changing the channel while still sitting was a remote possibility.

My plan is to do nothing today. I'm auditioning for American Idle.

I lost my watch. I meant to look for it, but I never found the time.

I didn't think I needed a leather jacket, but eventually I was suede.

I'm bad at wrapping presents. I just don't have the gift.

My company developed a revolutionary new broom. It's sweeping the nation.

Abstinence leave a lot to be desired.

The pyromaniac was careless and made an ash of himself.

Now that my best friend is on a diet, I'm seeing a lot less of him.

My friend dug a hole in my backyard until he hit water. I was annoyed, but I know he meant well.

I have a story about my bed. I made it up.

The thief stole a case of laundry detergent and made a clean getaway.

Being boxed in, I couldn't get out of the parking space. I needed a backup plan.

There was a nerf shoot out at the T-shirt shop. So many causal-tees.

I was almost creamed by a runaway milk truck. It was udderly terrifying.

I frequently break into song, because I can't find the right key.

My neighbor was arrested for indecent exposure. The details were quite revealing.

A case of underwear was stolen off a loading dock. Police made a brief inquiry.

Beautiful lawns are highly sod after.

When traveling from Russia to Alaska, it's important to get your Bering Strait.

I hurt my hand punching a computer monitor and had to call tech knuckle support.

I found a lot of unfriendly inns in Europe. It was a hostel environment.

I fall off my bike a lot but I keep getting back on. I believe in recycling.

My affair with art started in Paris. It was Louvre at first sight.

I drew the curtains in my room, but the rest of the furniture was real.

I'd like to visit Holland someday, wooden shoe?

I was over thinking the new fence. A clear cut case of not being able to cedar wood for the trees.

I went to a police auction. It was a complete bust.

My wife says I'm like a volcano in bed. Dormant.

I'm very good with spreadsheets. You could say I Excel at them.

The city council has to decide between a reservoir or an indoor arena. Their dammed if they do and domed if they can't.

My friend accidentally sawed off his left hand, but the doctor said he'd be all right.

We're near the end of the foggy season. When it's gone it won't be mist.

As much as I tried to push the envelope, it was still stationary.

Disturbing burial plots has grave consequences.

Jokes about airplanes go over my head.

I hope I never lose my legs. I couldn't stand it.

I asked the contractor how much for a new roof. He told me it was on the house.

As she exited the tattoo parlor, I knew she was trouble. It was written all over her.

There are lots of dangerous cults out there. Remember to practice safe sects.

Beats me why anyone would want to be a masochist.

My computer is so old and slow, it hertz.

I once auditioned for a part with a flute. I blew it.

The department store had a contest for the best mannequin. The competition was stiff.

The sign on the perfume counter said, “out of odor.”

Why do people write on birthday cakes? Because everyone wants to have their cake and read it too.

I have two shoes, but one of them isn’t right.

I went to a still life art exhibit, but it wasn’t moving.

Never ask someone to cut you some slack, when bungee jumping.

My favorite color is purple. I like it better than blue and red combined.

Two hats hung in the hallway, one says to the other, “You stay here. I’ll go on a head.”

Unveiling the statue wasn't just a big deal, it was monumental.

My brother and I may be rivals, but it's all relative.

If the devil went bald, there will be hell toupee.

Red, white, and blue stand for freedom, unless they're behind you.

If you can't live without your phone, you're a prisoner to it. A cell phone.

When I die I want my ashes spread in every country, but that's me all over.

Napoleon may not have designed his shirt, but he had a hand in it.

It's takes five minutes to get to the bar near my house, but thirty-five to get back. The difference is staggering.

If you put your left shoe on the wrong foot, it's on the right foot.

The popularity of glass coffins remains to be seen.

My Dad is slowly going bald. Hair today, gone tomorrow.

Steam engines get coaled in the winter.

At any time, the urge to sing The Lion Sleeps Tonight is only a whim away. A whim away, a whim away, a whim away...

About the Author

TH Leatherman is a writer from Firestone, Colorado. He enjoys humor, science fiction, fantasy, wine making, and the Rocky Mountain lifestyle. When not busy writing his next book, he can be found hiking with his wife and two sons, or walking his rescued dogs. He graduated Summa Cum Laude from Regis University with a degree in Business Management and a minor in Psychology.

Connect with Mr. Leatherman

Check out his blog and links to other books – psst. There's also a free book if you sign up for his mailing list.

https://thleatherman.com/

More puns, jokes, and one-liners

https://www.facebook.com/TH-Leatherman

@thleatherman on Twitter

TH.Leatherman on Instagram

Can't get enough stories by TH Leatherman? New chapters of exclusive stories are posted every other week on his Patreon page.

https://www.patreon.com/THLeatherman

Check out TH Leatherman's YouTube Channel for weekly videos. Author interviews, book reviews, and tips for writers.

https://www.youtube.com/channel/UCpB5ygo4EBYzt3V8XXyyrHQ

Reviews!

Authors (especially me) love reviews. Good, bad, or indifferent tell me what you think. You can do it easily on Amazon and Goodreads, but anywhere book lovers congregate is appreciated.